The Unobtainable Man

Harriet Wheatley

BookLeaf Publishing

Presentation by *BookLeaf Publishing*

Web: www.bookleafpub.com

E-mail: info@bookleafpub.com

ISBN : 9789394788114

First edition 2022

DEDICATION

This short book of poems is dedicated to my unobtainable love.

A little side note to my Grandma Elwyn, who always wanted a book dedicated to her, this ones for you Grandma!

ACKNOWLEDGEMENT

Thank you to my small circle of people for inspiring me always.

My family, my loves, my friends and mother nature.

PREFACE

"Be strong enough to let go and wise enough to
wait for what you deserve" - Anon

Everything

To me he is everything,
The flame in the torch
And the light in the night.
The guide in the stars
And the path through the trees.
The parts of me that have never loved
Ache for him,
And the parts of me that have always loved
Don't matter.

Why him?

I wouldn't draw him in school.
When you map out what your life looks like,
I know,
It wouldn't have been him.
And honestly?
It still wouldn't be him.
Sometimes I wish it wasn't him;
The all and everything I never wanted,
Yet suddenly it's him....
The all and everything I want.

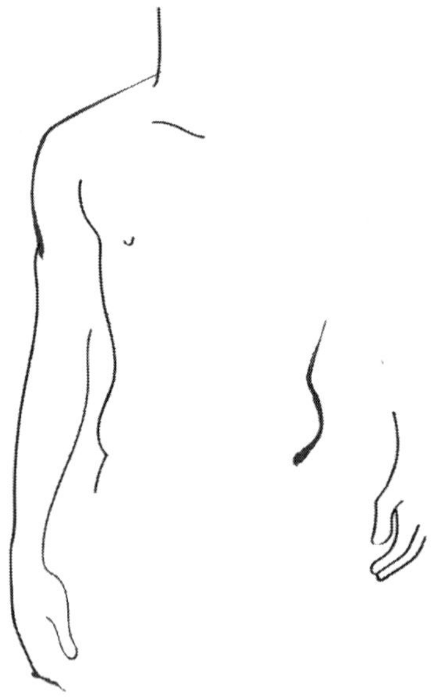

Determined

The man I love walks away from me more often
than he walks towards me.
He sees me for who I am but I cannot see him.
There are barriers and bumps in the road and we
haven't even started the journey;
Damned before it can begin
But there is no stopping me now.

How I Know

To know how you feel is a challenge
but there is one way for me.
I picture our life with nothing,
All that that life would be;
No flavour, no decoration,
Just us.
All wild and free.
The life I will still be choosing,
Is the one when you're with me.

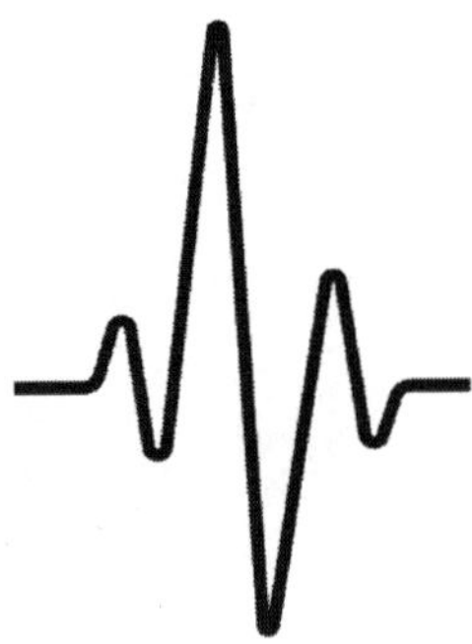

Sitting pretty, catching dust

How long will I be sat, just waiting,
Sitting pretty, catching dust.
When will you stop time for me,
Prove this isn't lust.
I think about you too much
but still my needs come first.
I'm ready for our life now
Or are these feelings cursed?

Matters of the heart

I feel like you believe in us, and you and me.
I know you can't just leave
But we are meant to be.
I'm not the only one that's waiting
For my life to start
But I am the one debating,
Matters of the heart.

Wise

Wise in ways you would not know,
No step too high, no step too low.
He comes and goes...
But after that
His arms are open
And you're back
In the place where you belong;
Just me and you and our song.

The Miss of the Mountains

For now I explore on my own,
Listening to the old songs,
Watching the sunrise.
My God looks different to yours,
Yours is fading.
Mine is covered in leafy green patterns,
Surrounded by dainty bright flowers.
She smiles,
She blows the light my way,
She believes in us, My God.
She tells me it's okay to be inspired.
Not God in the traditional sense,
For she is a God;
A Goddess,
The Miss of the Mountains,
Mother nature,
The other half of my heart.

The Spark

One day I hope I find out
Where I stand in your heart?
A friend?
A bystander?
The phone calls meant something.
The spark did not only ignite on my side of the
fence.
You felt it
But you hold back.
And I get that.
But one day,
I want to be the one.

The one that lets you fall back in love
With yourself, the world, nature and us.

Light Beams

The future I do not imagine in such detail with
anybody else.
The venue, the dress, the details - they do not
matter.
With you the vision is full of life;
Green trees in the breeze,
Light beaming through the forest,
Bright, white and deserving of it.
Many moments in my mind have lead to this;
Someone who does not want marriage,
Someone who does not want children,
Someone who suddenly fantasizes about both...
Only with you.

The smile I thought had given up

On the darkest days
You bring the sunshine,
The smile I thought had given up.
My worries, somewhere else.
For a brief moment you are all I see,
The world through your eyes
Is all I need.

Save us

The fire I watch ignite inside you,
A man of passion and temper.
You care...
You care too much,
Protecting everyone.
The hands that can cure,
The smile that can heal,
The stance of strength,
The white rock,
The pillar of sturdiness.
Save me,
Save us.
Hold me,
Hold us.
Shield us from the wounds of Earth,
The day-to-day that makes things worse,
Boldly go and live your life
Maybe then I'll be your wife.

Prince or not.

The story is as old as time,
No princess here for you to find.
All of me is what you'll get,
Nothing more, nothing less.
All the frogs have been kissed,
None that I can say I've missed.
Prince or not,
You're all I want-
I love you, in swirling font.

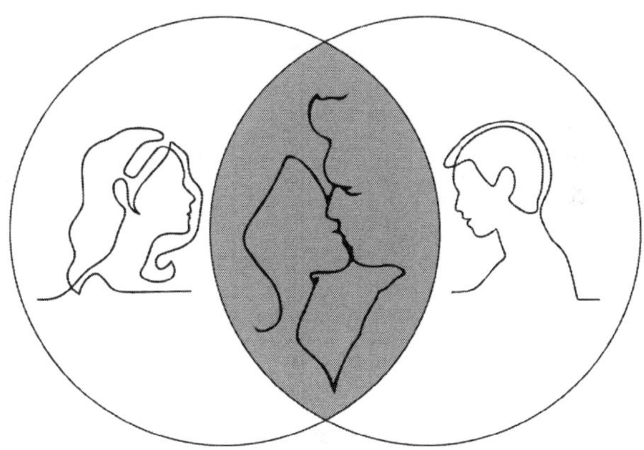

The warmth of one

Calm is the night
And warm are the hearts,
The hearts that start
The fire of others.
The burn that turns
The cogs of life,
Life that starts
When parts ignite.
The warmth of one
Spreads love to many,
The warmth of one,
Fills the soul.
The warmth of one
Spreads love to many.
The warmth of one
Makes us feel whole.
The love of one
Burns strong within.

To Know You

You are there,
An arm reach away,
"It's not like that" I say.
It isn't the bed that I want
or the life or the money,
I just want to hold your hand.
Hold your hand and watch you smile.
You aren't the reward,
The reward is knowing you.
I am so lucky just to know you,
That surely makes me greedy.
The ugly human trait that ensures we always
need more.
Perhaps I am happier holding on to the dream
But I think the dream would be happier, if it
were real.

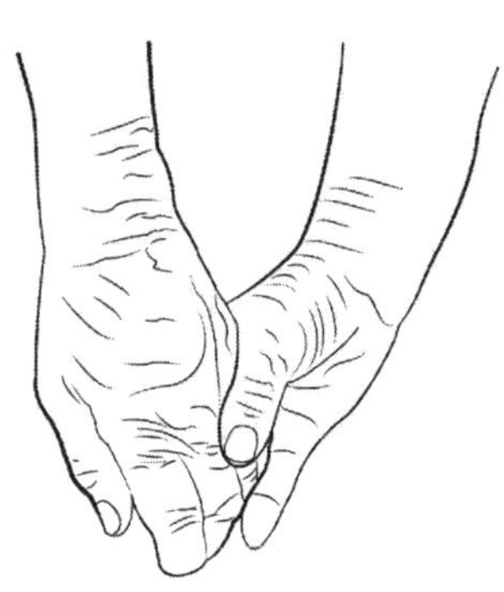

How wrong I was

When I close my eyes and think of you,
There you are in slow motion.
When the world moves so fast
There you are grounding me.
A player I thought,
How wrong I was.
Unintelligent I thought;
You proved me wrong.
Just a crush I thought,
One year later, how wrong I was.

Until you

The parts I miss;
Your palm,
Your brow,
When you laugh,
Like really laugh;
I can think of nothing else.
"You are deep", he says.
He sees straight into me.
What separates us, threads us,
Weaves between our bond.
You aren't always there,
Which I can't always bear.
You have this presence,
One that I can't explain.
Never have I wanted
To give someone everything,
Until you.

Quiet Moments

Quiet moments,
You and me.
Little noises,
We can't see.
Each walk of life
We have been through,
All of this
Feels so new.

The story we begin to tell

Be still my heart,
Be still my mind,
Our love was not so greatly timed.
Wait we did
And live we will,
The story we begin to tell...

We did it

Its you and me, we did it,
We took the leap of faith.
Now hold my hand forever
Until your dying days.
Those eyes show me your journey,
How far you've come alone.
Your smile is not so lost now,
Don't worry, you are home.

After all

Bold and whole,
The strongest one.
His mind lifts too,
The clever one,
The one that I am proud to call
My happy ever after,
After all.